HIGH-TECH AND PROGRAMMING
Careers in the Gig Economy

Celia McCarty

San Diego, CA

About the Author

Celia McCarty is a writer and editor in technical and educational fields. She worked with teens and young adults as a social worker and para-educator.

© 2024 ReferencePoint Press, Inc.
Printed in the United States

For more information, contact:
ReferencePoint Press, Inc.
PO Box 27779
San Diego, CA 92198
www.ReferencePointPress.com

ALL RIGHTS RESERVED.
No part of this work covered by the copyright hereon may be reproduced or used in any form or by any means—graphic, electronic, or mechanical, including photocopying, recording, taping, web distribution, or information storage retrieval systems—without the written permission of the publisher.

Picture Credits:
Cover: Dragon Images/Shutterstock

5: Maury Aaseng
8: VideoBCN/Shutterstock
11: SDI Productions/iStock
14: Charles Brutlag/Shutterstock
17: ESB Professional/Shutterstock
19: Shalstock/Shutterstock
24: Nopparat Khokthong/Shutterstock

28: Lucky Business/Shutterstock
31: Ljupco Smokovski/Shutterstock
33: Ground Picture/Shutterstock
36: Creativa Images/Shutterstock
39: Ground Picture/Shutterstock
42: Ceri Breeze/Shutterstock
46: Gorodenkoff/Shutterstock
49: Uladzik Kryhin/Shutterstock
51: Mila Supinskaya Glashchenko/Shutterstock

LIBRARY OF CONGRESS CATALOGING-IN-PUBLICATION DATA

Names: McCarty, Celia, author.
Title: High-tech and programming careers in the gig economy / by Celia McCarty.
Description: San Diego, CA : ReferencePoint Press, 2024. | Series: Careers in the gig economy | Includes bibliographical references and index.
Identifiers: LCCN 2023005013 (print) | LCCN 2023005014 (ebook) | ISBN 9781678205263 (library binding) | ISBN 9781678205270 (ebook)
Subjects: LCSH: Science--Vocational guidance--Juvenile literature. | Computer science--Vocational guidance--Juvenile literature. | High technology industries--Juvenile literature. | Gig economy--Juvenile literature.
Classification: LCC Q147 .M336 2024 (print) | LCC Q147 (ebook) | DDC 502.3--dc23/eng20230415
LC record available at https://lccn.loc.gov/2023005013
LC ebook record available at https://lccn.loc.gov/2023005014

CONTENTS

Introduction   **4**
Gig Work in High Tech and Programming

Chapter One   **7**
Tech Work in the Gig Economy

Chapter Two   **16**
Breaking into the High-Tech and
Programming Gig Economy

Chapter Three   **26**
The Upsides of Gig Work

Chapter Four   **35**
The Downsides of Gig Work

Chapter Five   **44**
Making a Go of It

Source Notes	53
Interview with a Solutions/Software Architect	56
Find Out More	58
Index	62

INTRODUCTION

Gig Work in High Tech and Programming

The tech industry experienced convulsions in 2022 and early 2023. Dozens of tech companies, large and small, laid off thousands of tech workers. Industry experts say they expect a couple of rocky years, but most agree that the tech industry will bounce back. Even in the midst of this turmoil, writers Heather Joslyn and Jennifer Riggins note, "there are still far more open positions than people to fill them."[1]

While some of these positions—and others—will be reserved for employees, there is also ongoing interest in hiring gig workers. These are the workers who have traditionally been known as freelancers, contract workers, or independent contractors. Nowadays they're also called gig workers. The term *gig* came from the music world. When a band or musician performs, it is called a "gig." Originally, musicians played for an evening and then the club owner paid them—in cash. In the gig economy a tech worker might complete a short-term project or longer-term contract in exchange for money. While gig work can be associated with low-wage platform-dependent work, there is also a high-paying niche for high-tech and programming professionals.

The Rise of Independent Work

Lindsay Hodgson is one of these professionals. As a software consultant, she installs and maintains medical records software for hospitals. After contributing to the development of the software as a software company employee, she quit to become an independent contractor in the gig economy. "I feel like I've sort of achieved my version of the American dream," she says. "I'm not looking to make any changes to my situation. I'm very happy."[2]

The "gig economy" is a new name for the part of the workforce that is not in traditional employment. As the number of people in alternative work arrangements grows, this type of labor participation is a factor in the overall economy. It is not a new form of work, just a time-honored way of earning money with a new

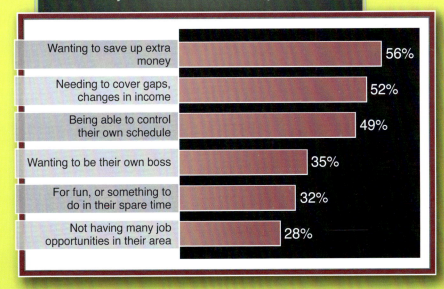

What Draws People to Gig Work?

Increasing savings and filling in gaps in income are the top two reasons given for working at gig jobs. This was the finding of a 2021 Pew Research Center survey that sought to understand why people are drawn to gig work. The next most common reason cited for gig work was flexible scheduling.

% of current or recent gig workers who say each of the following is a *major* reason why they have taken on these jobs

Wanting to save up extra money	56%
Needing to cover gaps, changes in income	52%
Being able to control their own schedule	49%
Wanting to be their own boss	35%
For fun, or something to do in their spare time	32%
Not having many job opportunities in their area	28%

Source: Monica Anderson et al., "The State of Gig Work in 2021," Pew Research Center, December 8, 2021. www.pewresearch.org.

name. What is new is how many people and businesses are involved and the way that technology continues to make it easier to untether from an office location. Technology makes remote work possible and finding clients easier. Freelancers can often interview online and take on projects potentially from anywhere. Mindful of the responsibilities of self-employment, tech workers can make the gig economy work for them.

Why Wait?

Many people in high tech and programming careers started in their teens. If you have the interest, there are so many ways to gain knowledge and expertise, whether at school through classes and clubs, or with friends, hackathons, or your own personal projects. And once you are sixteen years old or have a work permit, there are legitimate opportunities to begin earning money. Those first jobs might not go smoothly, but they will likely provide valuable lessons for the future.

This was the experience of one Reddit user, who describes a first gig job this way:

As a senior in high school I decided to try out freelance work. My first job I was tasked to debug an Android application written in Lua. I thought that it would be a quick hour long job. Little did I know the horrors I would uncover in that code base. I bid 30 dollars, and got the job. As I started to explore the code base, I saw programming nightmares that still haunt me to this day, extreme spaghetti code, poor naming conventions and an over use of global variables made the project an absolute nightmare. The debugging job took me a solid 3, 8 hour days. Debugging was a nightmare because of the way the project was setup, I couldn't use ADB [Android Debug Bridge] or nearly any other Android tools. Safe to say, this was a fantastic learning experience.[3]

CHAPTER ONE

Tech Work in the Gig Economy

Chances are, if you are interested in high-tech and programming careers, a good part of what would appeal to you in a job are encountering intellectual challenges and finding ways to solve real-world problems. In addition to interesting work, tech gigs have the advantage of being better paid and offering more flexibility than gig work in other fields. But although gig work provides flexibility and autonomy, it can be less stable than traditional employment.

What Are High-Tech and Programming Jobs?

The Bureau of Labor Statistics places high-tech and programming jobs in the category "professional, scientific, and technical services." There are many high-tech jobs in this category, and overall they are projected to grow faster than the average over the next ten years. In 2022 Glassdoor, a job search site, listed what it describes as the "Best Jobs in America." This list is based on the number of openings, pay, and job satisfaction. Eight of its top ten jobs in 2022 were in tech: enterprise architect, full stack engineer, data scientist, development and operations engineer, machine learning engineer, data engineer, software engineer, and Java developer. Many fields—such as cloud engineering, artificial intelligence (AI), and information security—are expected to continue to

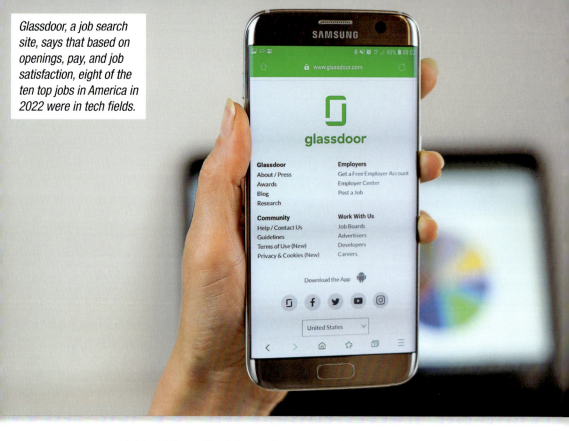

Glassdoor, a job search site, says that based on openings, pay, and job satisfaction, eight of the ten top jobs in America in 2022 were in tech fields.

grow quickly. What all of these jobs have in common is a science, technology, engineering, and math (STEM) background.

Cybersecurity is one example of a high-tech field. Cybersecurity engineers work to keep information safe from hackers. There is a shortage of people with the skills needed to work in information security, a high-pressure field. US employers have long struggled to fill cybersecurity positions. According to a 2022 study led by the National Initiative for Cybersecurity Education (NICE), in 2022 there were fifty-three thousand open positions.

What They Do

High-tech workers and programmers create and modify applications and systems to meet a client's needs. There is a wide variety of work that these knowledge workers perform. They may modify an off-the-shelf accounting program for a company, research mathematical models for simulating blood flow, structure data for analysis, create video game special effects, or help build a new robotic product.

Data science is a hot field right now. It involves working with collections of data, often called data sets. Data sets are electronic information files. Examples of a data set include US Census information about millions of Americans, or seismic (earthquake) activity records of magnitude, energy release, and shaking intensity over time. Data sets can be in many forms, including images, videos, and sound. These data sets can be valuable sources of information. Data scientists can apply statistical analysis to spot

Building Résumés and Community with STEM Projects

Projects can be a great way to build knowledge and experience in high-tech fields. Assistive technology is an example of high tech that draws from science, technology, engineering, math, and design. At the Western New York (WNY) STEM Hub free summer program in 2021, students built a prosthetic hand for seven-year-old Josiah. High school senior Elias Humphrey describes seeing Josiah wear the hand they built: "To see him now and bring his idea to life with the colors he wanted and everything, it's very impactful. I want to be a mechanical engineer. This helps me run the mechanics and use 3-D printers."

Ninety students at a Minnesota high school worked in groups on designs for assistive technology to make walking easier for Sadie, a dog who had lost one leg in an accident. The students really connected with Sadie and their goal of helping her be more mobile. As high school junior Sam Doughty notes, "Everyone working together is always a great thing."

Participating in projects like these not only builds a résumé for school applications and jobs, it can build community and help others.

Quoted in Alexa Imani Spencer, "High School Students Build a Prosthetic Hand for 7-Year-Old Boy," Black Enterprise, August 19, 2021. www.blackenterprise.com.

Quoted in Sydney Page, "A 3-Legged Dog Was Struggling. A High School Engineering Class Stepped In," *Washington Post*, February 15, 2023. www.washingtonpost.com.

patterns. For example, data scientists can explore health records (with identifying information removed) to uncover trends, such as regions where people have higher-than-average cancer rates. Then government and nonprofits determine causes and solutions.

Larry W., a research mathematician, uses math to draw useful insights from large data sets. He says, "I do a lot of statistical modeling of data. My day is a lot of computer programming."[4] Creating statistical models or algorithms that analyze data and make predictions based on the data is a type of machine learning.

Machine learning is a tool used to automate data analysis. As a simple example, school districts could employ machine learning to analyze what students order from the school lunch menu. They could learn what items are the most popular and could even determine what items are most popular on which day of the week, or they could compare this data to the weather and temperature to determine that more drinks are sold when the temperature soars. This information would allow those providing school meals to better align with student buying behavior.

Machine learning engineer Daniel Bourke did a project in a field of AI called computer vision. The data he had was in the form of images. The client gave Bourke an example of the type of information being sought from the image data set. Bourke explains, "There was some sort of issue in a park and someone took a photo of it and submitted it. Could we use that image to figure out what was the issue that person was submitting?"[5] In this case, Bourke was not successful. It turned out that because the images were all so different and each image had multiple labels, this was not an issue that machine learning could solve.

Other types of careers focus on understanding how people use tech or how programs affect people. Heather is a user experience (UX) researcher. She says, "My job involves talking to people and finding out what they like and don't like about the programs they're using. I look at processes, how someone is learning some-

Machine learning, a tool used to automate data analysis, can be used to keep track of the most popular items on a school's lunch menu.

thing, how they use a program." Usually, she researches tech products. But for one project, she says, "I looked at how returning to the office after Covid19 worked for people." She uses research techniques like user interviews as well as other tools, explaining, "Sometimes we just talk to people and ask them, sometimes we watch people, we observe them to see what type of issues they run into, sometimes we use surveys to determine how well they like things. . . . I work remotely [but] I have gone onsite to observe people running and riding bikes as they try out different kinds of hardware. It is a great job."[6]

Autonomy Means Being Resourceful

What a tech worker does will vary with the job, and since gigs are short term, the work can be more clearly defined. Nick D., a technical writer, has worked both as an independent contractor and in traditional full-time jobs. As a contractor, he says, "you're given a lot of autonomy . . . you're given a job, you're told to work on it, you're given a little bit of assistance but not a ton. You often don't have the downsides of being a full-time employee. Like all the company meetings. . . . There's a lot of being left on your own to do the work you're given and as long as you're doing that work well, that's pretty well regarded."[7]

As a freelancer, you may be working on things that are new to you. And you might have to be very resourceful because clients often assume that you already know what you're doing even though every project is different. Web developer Brad Traversy shares, "I can tell you from my experience that I had very very few projects where the client explained what they wanted and it just popped right in my head what I was gonna

Working with New Problems That No One's Figured Out

People in high-tech and programming careers are problem solvers. Sometimes they are addressing new problems that no one's figured out. A research mathematician uses math to solve a wide range of problems. This can include using data science and machine learning. There are prebuilt software packages, but for a new problem, an engineer or mathematician must create a statistical model and then determine how to train it. For example, if the problem is understanding why there is a prevalence of a certain cancer in a region, the mathematician or engineer determines how to train the model. Training entails feeding data—in this case health records and other data such as the presence of hazardous chemicals in the region—into the model. Research mathematician Larry W. says that what he finds appealing is assessing "what's the right type of statistical model? How do you train it? Can you get it to train faster? Or, how much better will the model be if I train it longer? Or, if I use this training method vs. that training method, how can I trade off speed or time for better performance?"

Larry W., interview with the author, January 10, 2023.

do. I have to do a lot of research and figure out what technologies, what plugins I'm gonna use, things like that, and I just figured it out as I went along."[8]

How Much Do Tech Jobs Typically Pay?

Tech careers typically pay higher than most. Knowing what tech employees are paid can be a starting point for evaluating gig rates. Pay varies somewhat across the United States, with experience, and by company. According to the job search website Indeed, salaries for data scientists average $123,750, for software engineers $109,120, and for machine learning engineers $149,660, According to the job search website ZipRecruiter, AI engineers' salaries average $156,650. In addition to salaries, it is not unusual for tech workers to receive stock options, cash bonuses, and other incentives.

Since the pandemic there has been a tight labor market for tech workers, with many more jobs than people to fill them. The big tech company layoffs have released a lot of highly qualified people into the job market, making it possible for some smaller organizations and government agencies to hire newly available top-tier tech talent as employees and for short-term projects, or gigs. Nonprofits are benefiting too. Since the pandemic, nonprofits have experienced an increase in tech candidates. Noah Hart, founder of the job board Tech Jobs for Good, notes, "There's been a longer trend of more and more job seekers looking for impactful roles. A lot of organizations are still hiring and are getting a lot more applications."[9]

Generally, gig workers are paid by the hour or by the project. Their pay may be a bit higher than that of an employee's because they have expenses, such as paying for their own health care. Go Remotely, a job board for international remote work, says average pay for AI gigs is $115 per hour, and blockchain architecture pays

Amazon's voice assistant, Alexa, uses natural language processing to answer many spoken queries.

$87 per hour. Blockchain architecture is a way of structuring valuable encrypted data that makes it more secure. Average hourly pay for robotics is $77 per hour, and virtual reality is $50 per hour.

How Stable and Reliable Are Tech Gigs?

Since for freelancers the gig ends once the contract term completes or the project is finished, they may face more instability than a permanent employee. Generally, demand is strong for positions in these fields, though economic downturns do occur, leading to layoffs. In the downturn that began in 2022, many who were laid off by big tech companies such as Google and Microsoft are reportedly finding work freelancing or as employees. Some are taking the opportunity to work for government, nonprofits, and smaller companies. And some are moving to industries such as finance, insurance, and transportation.

As mass layoffs demonstrate, nothing is permanent. Many tech workers learned that they cannot count on a company to provide them with secure employment. Tech workers are a type of knowledge worker. Knowledge workers conceive and execute work to develop and deliver products and services. In a survey of five hundred knowledge workers in the United States, published in January 2023 by *Fast Company* and Pollfish, 74 percent of respondents said that the recent waves of layoffs made freelance work more attractive than before.

CHAPTER TWO

Breaking into the High-Tech and Programming Gig Economy

Whether doing traditional or gig work, the process of preparing for high-tech and programming careers is similar. Education and experience are key. Once you are ready, a combination of telling people you are available and researching and applying online is how most people find work.

Start Learning Now

High-level tech work typically requires a lot of education. Successful techs come from many educational backgrounds. You can begin preparing by taking advantage of STEM classes offered in middle school and high school. Larry W., a research mathematician, suggests, "I would encourage people to take a statistics class and a programming class when they're in high school. It gets you thinking in a different way than the traditional math classes. Thinking about how to tell a computer what to do is a good skill to have to be the master of the computer instead of it telling you what your choices are."[10]

If you struggle a bit with STEM classes, you are not the only one. Seek out help from your teachers, counselors, librarians, friends, and family when you need it. Form a study group with other students. Look for useful websites that can help you study online. One of these is Khan Academy, which offers free online courses in middle and high school math, statistics, and science, as well as coding and computer science. Being able to reach out to others for help, collaborate with others, and do your own research and study are all skills you will use in any career.

Summer Opportunities

Taking summer courses at a community college or university may be an option. In addition, some universities offer summer programs for high school students. There are many types of programs in many high-tech fields. Students must apply and be selected in order to attend and most include on-campus stays of a week or two. For those who love math, universities host high-level summer math programs. These programs open a new world, exposing students to "this idea that the problems aren't all solved—there's room to discover new things,"[11] notes Larry W. Programs

Teachers, counselors, and librarians are all excellent resources for anyone who struggles with STEM classes.

for strong students in math include Boston University's Program in Mathematics for Young Scientists, the University of Chicago's Young Scholars Program, and the Ross Mathematics Program in Indiana.

And there are many other programs for high school students, like Howard University's High School Summer Enrichment Programs. Howard is a historically Black university. In 2023 Information Systems, Actuarial Science, and Entrepreneurship were three of the offerings in its summer enrichment programs. The National Initiative for Cybersecurity Education summer internship program and the WNY STEM Hub summer and after-school programs are other examples. There are many more. Research online and check with your teachers, school counselor, or librarian.

College and Internships

Most high-tech jobs ask for at least a bachelor's degree, and many look for a master's degree. In some fields, a doctorate or postdoctoral work is needed. Common degrees are in electrical engineering, computer science, and software engineering. College students often have the opportunity to apply for internships, during which they work for an organization to gain experience. An internship gives a student a chance to check out an organization and what it is like to work there. Some organizations will extend a job offer to interns after they graduate.

Skills and Certifications

As a student you can access some free online classes from places like freeCodeCamp, Google, LinkedIn Learning, or the public library. Tutorials, YouTube videos, online courses, and boot camps are some of the many ways techs learn and upgrade their skills. This effort can put a tech in a good position to move into a new field when the next hot technology appears—or even to create it.

Professionals can take tests to gain certification and demonstrate knowledge of products such as Amazon Web Services.

Professionals can earn industry-recognized certifications to demonstrate knowledge, such as for Amazon Web Services and Google Professional Cloud Architect products. The certification tests take an hour and a half to two hours and cost $100 to $300 each, depending on the level. Industry associations also provide certification, such as the Computing Technology Industry Association's most basic certification, which requires nine to twelve months of work experience and costs about $250 for the ninety-minute exam.

Experience

Clearly, some of this learning will have to wait until you're a little older and further along in your education or work life. But teens who have an aptitude for tech work and an interest in getting into this field, whether for gig work or full-time employment, can start getting experience early. Many young people build their own apps, take part in hackathons, or help friends or family members with

Build a Voice App

Building a voice app is one of the ways that students can practice tech skills and create something for their portfolio. Amazon's Alexa is a voice app; it responds to human voice commands. Steven Arkonovich built Big Sky, an Alexa app that provides weather reports, as a side project. People can ask the app to tell them what the high temperature will be that day or when the rain will start, for example. Arkonovich learned to code just to create the app.

Kesha Williams has been coding since high school. She has a degree in math and computer science. She says, "I love being a software engineer because I'm able to bring ideas to life." Voice technology interested her right away. She says, "Just the thought of talking to a computer and having it understand me was intriguing. That's what inspired me to play around with Alexa and learn how to build [apps]." So on the side of her full-time job, she built apps, like Live Plan Eat. "My kids are always asking me what's for dinner, and sometimes even I can't remember. So my first [app] was really just to make my life easier."

Quoted in Jennifer King, "Kesha Williams, a Seasoned IT Professional, Proves Alexa Has a Place in Business Technology," Alexa Blogs, Amazon, February 15, 2018. https://developer.amazon.com.

websites. In addition, Adam Sinicki, a freelance software developer, suggests "getting involved in open-source projects on GitHub, or . . . you could build your own app, upload it to the [Google] Play Store, and then generate a passive income from it."[12] When Sinicki refers to passive income, he is talking about earning money on a regular basis from something you created. Every time someone purchases your app on the Play Store, you receive a portion of the sale price without having to do any additional work on that app.

Projects that you create can become part of a portfolio, which is a collection of samples of your work that are online or that you can email to others. This will become important once you start looking for work. People looking for full-time employment or gig work in the tech fields are often asked to show samples of their work.

Finding Work

Many techs find work through people they know. When they let friends, family, professors, and professional contacts know that they are available for work, this is called networking. Alex Suzuki is a software engineer. He shares advice for finding your first freelance client:

> Nothing beats a network of real-life industry contacts. . . . I've met many different people during my first couple of years as an employee, some of them customers, most of them fellow co-workers. They went on to work for other companies, or built even their own, and we kept in touch. Many of them are now in management-level positions— potential customers and door-openers.[13]

Job Scams

Aside from the network of people they know, many techs find work online. With online jobs, take the time to check them out before sharing sensitive information. Posting fake jobs is a way for scammers to gather personal information, such as Social Security numbers (SSNs). Some even ask for money. If a job posting says it is for a legitimate organization, don't click on links in the posting or email. Instead, search for the company's legitimate web page to find the job.

Even someone with a master's degree in human resources can be fooled by job scams, as Keren1986 shared on Reddit:

> I fell completely for a fake job offer. They used a real company and real employee names. The emails looked real . . . and they sent me a job offer letter and W-4 form which I stupidly filled out and now they have my SSN. It wasn't until they told me I had to wire money to get the equipment

needed for training that I realized it was a scam. I even talked to them on the phone. I thought it was real. . . . I told my friends and family that I landed a great job. I've since put a credit freeze on myself since they have my social. . . . I deleted my LinkedIn and Indeed profiles.[14]

Freelancing Platforms

While they are building up their network, some techs find gig work on gig platforms. These are sites where potential clients list projects and what they are willing to pay for the project. The platform may also track your hours, process work through the platform on the client's behalf, bill the client, and pay you—in exchange for a fee. Sites like Toptal, Crossover, Upwork, and Freelancer connect workers with jobs. Some platforms don't allow you to look at jobs or what the jobs pay unless you sign up. It is a good idea to research a gig platform's reviews. Generally, the pay is lower than when working directly for a client, because the platform keeps part of what the client pays. Toptal requires an intensive testing process for techs, which includes tech knowledge as well as soft skills, such as communication and professionalism. The platform says its screening allows it to accept only top talent—the origin of the name Toptal. Toptal doesn't disclose its rates, but online reviews say that on average, full-stack developers are paid $70 to $120 per hour in North America. Full-stack developers have the knowledge to work on all aspects of a website. In comparison, reviewers say Upwork's average pay for full-stack developers is $40 to $100 per hour, but Upwork takes a portion of that. For each gig, Upwork takes 20 percent of the first $500, 10 percent after that up to $10,000 in earnings, and 5 percent of anything beyond that.

Be careful with all online job postings, even on gig platforms. A Reddit commenter shared, "I had someone on Upwork try to

Using LinkedIn

As a freelancer you're working on short-term contracts, so along with doing the work, you spend time finding work. Heather, a UX researcher, notes, "If you're really gigging, it is up to you—you're drumming up business all the time." She's discovered that LinkedIn is a useful tool to find gigs. Heather says, "I tend to go through LinkedIn because that's where people hire from. On LinkedIn people looking for certain skills will contact you."

Recruiters are people whose job it is to find workers for open positions. Recruiters search LinkedIn to find people with specific skill sets and reach out to them. Even when a freelancer is busy with gigs, it makes sense for him or her to talk with people offering work. Heather notes, "If people are interested in hiring me, I'm talking with them. You should always be acting like an entrepreneur." An updated profile and work sample help attract recruiters. Connecting with others in your field and professionally commenting on their posts can help. Heather adds, "Have a high-visibility post about what you're doing. Make yourself easy to find, make lots of connections."

Heather, interview with the author, January 8, 2023.

scam me. It seemed legit in the beginning. The person trying to scam me pretended they were from Procter and Gamble. They were going to send me equipment. Then they asked me to buy a couple of pieces. That is when I knew it was a scam."[15]

Some gig platforms do more than charge fees for their services. Some actually monitor the freelancer's workday. The platform Crossover was called out by a former gig worker on Glassdoor for its Work Smart surveillance system: "You must download a screen recorder/tracker—it monitors what you do while you're working, and takes screenshots of both you and your screen every ten minutes."[16]

There are many types of job search platforms, and some specialize. Freelancer caters to smaller clients and can be a good place for those with little experience. People post the projects they want done, and freelancers bid on them. Braintrust began as a freelancer community marketplace. Techs set their own fees, and the client pays an additional 10 percent to Braintrust.

Job Boards and Reverse Job Boards

Job boards are sites with listings of available jobs. Some sites specialize in gig work or tech work. All Tech Is Human, US Digital Response, Stack Overflow, and Tech Jobs for Good are examples of sites that cater to high-tech and other professionals. Reverse job boards offer a place for people to post their profiles for free and a way for those with projects to contact them. Some boards cater to a specific audience, those with specific skills, or a certain location. Hired is a reverse job board for software developers, and PythonDevs and RailsDevs are reverse job boards for people who work with Python and Rails programming languages.

LinkedIn is a job board, reverse job board, and professional networking site and is a prime source of work for many professionals.

LinkedIn

LinkedIn is a job board, reverse job board, and professional networking site. It is a prime source of work for many professionals. Workers list education, experience, credentials, and certifications and provide work samples on the site. There is opportunity to connect with others and to share photos, videos, and articles. Recruiters use the site to find and connect with people.

To break in to high-tech and programming careers, you can start to prepare now by taking STEM classes. Summer programs provide opportunities to explore your interests further. Take free online courses and earn certifications. Work on personal projects to gain experience and polish them as you build a portfolio of work samples for college applications or gig work. Once you are ready, let your network know you are looking for work and explore the job boards and freelancer platforms that interest you.

CHAPTER THREE

The Upsides of Gig Work

There are many upsides to working in the gig economy in high-tech fields. Gig work brings more freedom to choose whom you work for, what you do, and when and where you work. Being your own boss, being able to design your own work-life balance, having the opportunity to learn and work on a variety of projects, and having the potential for greater earning and job security are big pluses. Tech freelancer Adam Sinicki has thought about this and has no doubts: gig work is for him. He writes:

> Why spend hours commuting only to be given a fraction of the value you have provided the client or customer? Why feel forced to choose just one career or let someone else decide on your working hours and wages? Why work on projects you have no interest in? By offering services on a "per gig" basis, we free ourselves to select the kind of work that best serves our goals. We can use this to accelerate our careers and create a star-studded portfolio, or we can use it to design a lifestyle that lets us spend more time doing the things we love — with the people we love.[17]

The Benefit of Flexible Hours

Self-employed workers set their own schedules. They decide when to begin work, how long to work, and when to have breaks. As Sinicki says, "You'll be able to take days off when it suits you, or change your hours around as you see fit. You could work an extra two hours Monday to Thursday and take Fridays off. This is called 'lifestyle design,' which basically means fitting your job around your life, rather than the other way around."[18]

After leaving a full-time job as a machine learning team lead, Ethan Rosenthal shifted to gig work as a consulting data scientist. He appreciates the freedom this change has given him. When he worked a full-time job, he says,

> I would get to the gym in the morning, race through my workout, and then still have to shower and commute to the office. With consulting, I could work out in the morning, and then I would already be at the office. In the summertime, I could work from the gym's . . . outdoor cabanas that look out over the Hudson [River]. Once noon hit, the cabanas were no longer in the shade, so I would ride my bike home, clear my head on the ride, make some lunch, and work the rest of the afternoon, recharged, from home.[19]

A freelance tech professional can choose to make family, health, and well-being most important in their life. Sinicki notes, "I am never more appreciative that I work for myself than when my wife needs me to pick her up from work early because she's unwell. Being a freelancer lets me be there for the people I love."[20] That flexibility is critical for caregivers—people who are looking after children or family members with health issues. Heather shares that she left permanent employment to freelance because she

Self-employment offers the advantage of flexible schedules. Workers can decide when to begin work, how long to work, and when to take breaks.

"had a young kid who was being homeschooled, I could work when I wanted, and I could pick and choose what I wanted to do. It was the freedom of time to decide how much I wanted to work and how much time I wanted to spend with my family."[21]

Workplace Stress

The typical workplace can be stressful at times. Reporter Andrew Van Dam analyzed the comments of people who were interviewed by the Bureau of Labor Statistics about their typical workday. He found that "your workplace looms as the single most stressful place in the universe."[22]

According to Van Dam's analysis, finance and insurance industry workers report the most stress, followed by education and professional and technical workers. Those with STEM careers fall into this category of jobs with the second-highest stress level. Employed tech workers are subject to long hours, unpaid overtime, poor management, layoffs, and burnout. Independent workers have more autonomy, and they have choice in their working conditions.

The jobs with the least stress, according to this study, are those that require work outdoors in and around nature. High-tech gig workers can usually choose where they work and how much time they spend outdoors. This is one of the benefits of gig work: it allows outdoor time, whether the individual lives and works in a scenic setting or just sets up a work space near a window with a view of nature. Gig workers also have the flexibility to indulge in leisurely activities in nature, such as biking, hiking, swimming, kayaking, and even gardening.

Working Where You Want

A big benefit of many gig jobs is the ability to work remotely. One tech worker who has severe anxiety and obsessive-compulsive disorder says her conditions are "significantly exacerbated in an office setting." She reports that while working from home, her "mental health and performance vastly improved."[23]

Remote work can give neurodivergent individuals more freedom to flourish outside of conventional workplace expectations. One in fifteen people are neurodivergent, according to Centers for Disease Control and Prevention statistics. Neurodiversity looks at the way different people's brains work on a consistent basis. Some categories of neurological differences include autism, attention-deficit/hyperactivity disorder, dyslexia, and Tourette's syndrome, as well as some chronic mental health concerns like bipolar disorder, anxiety, and depression. Most workplaces are designed for neurotypical brains, with certain assumptions about how people should communicate and behave. When people act differently, there can be misunderstandings. This affects the ability of neurodivergent individuals to contribute professionally. According to Joseph Riddle, director of Neurodiversity in the Workplace, a business that fosters neurodiversity hiring, "Fewer than 1 in 6 neurodivergent job seekers are [working] full-time at the level they should be."[24]

Remote work provides other benefits to people, including those who live far from big cities or tech centers. After receiving her PhD, design research consultant Becca Kennedy found that "there weren't any local jobs that were a good match for me . . . so I created my own consulting company." She adds that it "has worked out amazingly well."[25]

When people don't have to go into an employer's office regularly, they have more freedom to choose where they live. People can choose to live someplace that has a lower cost of living, offers more outdoor activities, or is closer to family and friends. Hundreds of places in the United States are tempting digital nomads with

Extreme Flexibility

Tech workers who do gigs are running their own business. They determine when they will work in order to complete the contract. Technical writer Nick D. notes, "In the jobs I've worked as long as you get your work done nobody really cares when you work or how you work."

Online meetings may be the exception. Nick D. notes, "You have to be available for meetings. You have to be around for those hours, able to meet at a location where you can talk to people, but, in general meetings mostly are in the first half of the workday." Meetings can go overtime. Nick D. explains, "Sometimes I'll have a day where I have meetings from like 10:30 to 12:30, and I'll just have to jump off the call, go and grab some lunch. But everybody kind of gets that, that people will be off for a few minutes."

Aside from meetings, there is extreme flexibility. Nick D. notes, "You could do in principle 5 to 6 hours each day, include weekends and just take time off in the afternoons. You can kind of catch up one day and do lots another day."

Nick D., interview with the author, January 11, 2023.

Gig workers have the flexibility to enjoy time in nature, such as hiking, biking, or just taking the dog for a walk.

incentives to relocate there, including cash, money to purchase a home, and tax breaks. According to the website MakeMyMove, which lists cities that offer money to remote workers willing to relocate, Muncie, Indiana, offers $5,000 cash for relocation and touts its "small town college vibe," "big city amenities," "fresh local restaurants," "arts and entertainment," and "recreational opportunities." Make My Move's description of Montpelier, Vermont, entices readers with "more than just pretty landscapes, award-winning schools, a thriving small business environment, and Bernie Sanders." Remote workers can apply for "up to $5,000 per year for up to two years and applicants who move and become a full-time employee of a Vermont business are eligible for up to $7,500."[26] Digital nomads live and work internationally as well. Many countries—including Barbados, Croatia, Hungary, Iceland, Norway, and Portugal—offer visas and other incentives to attract digital nomads.

Remote Work Can Feel Safer

One of the benefits of being a tech freelancer is the ability to determine where one works. Journalist Karla Miller cites a recent study by Future Forum that indicates that working from home can feel safer for some. In majority White workplaces, people of other races and ethnicities may feel like they have to change the way they speak, dress, or act in order to be accepted. In addition, they may be subjected to microaggressions—subtle discrimination that can harm their mental health over time. The study found that "working at home has largely spared them from . . . having colleagues touch their hair; being mistaken for another colleague of the same race . . . overhearing insensitive commentary on or being pressured to discuss traumatizing news events such as racist violence."

Dealing with microaggressions and suppressing cultural identity in order to fit in can take a toll. Tina Gilbert, managing director of Management Leadership for Tomorrow, a partner of Future Forum, says that instead of having to "put a smile on your face and keep moving," working from home "means releasing that mental burden from people who are . . . getting paid to think."

Quoted in Karla L. Miller, "Microaggressions Like These at the Office Can Make Remote Work Even More Appealing," *Seattle Times*, May 17, 2021. www.seattletimes.com.

Meaningful Work

Gig work promises the ability to seek work that furthers personal and career interests. The freelancer decides whom they work for and what projects they work on. A 2018 *Harvard Business Review* study of the gig economy states:

> For most people in our study, striking out on their own initially involved doing whatever work would allow them to find a footing in the market. But they were adamant that succeeding means taking only work that clearly connects to a broader purpose. All could articulate why their work, or at least their best work—be it to empower women

through film, expose harmful marketing practices, sustain the American folk music tradition, or help corporate leaders succeed with integrity—is more than a means of earning a living.[27]

As a UX consultant, Becca Kennedy is able to follow her professional interests. She shares, "There are industries I'm drawn toward, like entertainment and wellness, and others that I prefer to avoid. I can also follow my curiosity in wild directions, whereas when you are a full-time researcher, you might be iterating on the same product or service for years."[28]

New Opportunities

A gig can be a chance to try a new job or industry and to gain new experience and skills, rounding out a résumé or portfolio. Technical writer Nick D. found that in comparison to full-time employment, "definitely one of the assets of contract jobs is it's easier to try

Gigs can give techs variety in their work as they can choose to work on different projects. Sometimes a three-month contract is a good way to see if you like a particular task.

things out for a bit, not commit yourself. [When] you're not positive a career is something you love, signing up for full-time job can be a little stressful. Signing up for a three-month contract isn't a bad way at all to try something out you might not try otherwise."[29]

Gigs can give techs variety in their work since they can choose to work on different projects. A software engineer commenting on Reddit as lhr0909 found a variety of gigs as a freelancer. He says he started

as a Java backend developer, but when I was free I would take frontend gigs on the side or build my own side projects with JavaScript full-stack. Once I started freelancing 3 years ago, I was able to take a big variety of projects on Upwork at the beginning to build a portfolio. Fast forward to now, I am running a team of freelancers (developers and designers) building [prototypes], and enterprise jobs [maintaining systems] from my local network and from Upwork with all kinds of technology.[30]

There are many upsides to freelancing in high-tech and programming careers. Software developer stardisgatetrekkie notes, "Programming isn't for everyone, but if you can learn it (hint: you can!) you'll literally open up a world of career possibilities worth getting excited about. I've been freelancing for 3 years now and absolutely love it. It's not easy but it's very interesting and fulfilling."[31]

CHAPTER FOUR

The Downsides of Gig Work

There are plenty of advantages to high-tech gig work, but there are also some disadvantages. Overcoming the downsides of gig work can help freelancers who work in high-tech fields find success.

Getting Work

Getting started in gig work can be challenging. It goes much more smoothly when you have a strong network of professional contacts, but developing that network takes time. Freelance software developer stardisgatetrekkie comments, "It's really hard to get freelancing momentum going from nothing (i.e. very little experience, no contacts in the tech industry, no past clients)." For those just starting out, stardisgatetrekkie suggests "freelancing on nights and weekends while the income you need to support yourself is coming from another job." That's a good way to get some experience, build a network of contacts, and still have money coming in. In time, good work will bring repeat clients and make it possible to earn a living in the gig economy. "But," stardisgatetrekkie cautions, "be prepared for it to take a few years before you're getting steady enough income from freelancing to quit your day job."[32]

A freelancer's biggest concern is often the uncertain income, After senior consultant Jon Munitz was laid off from IBM, he started freelancing. He has a yearlong contract, which offers some measure of security, but he has no way of knowing what will happen once the contract ends. "I definitely have the anxiety of not knowing when I can sign a lease"[33] on an apartment, he says.

The uncertainty that comes with gig work leads many freelancers to always be looking for the next gig. Mark Flory, a software development consultant, explains, "When I have work, I work a lot. . . . The one thing I do almost constantly . . . is search for work."[34] The constant need to search for or pitch new jobs can be stressful. Gig workers can spend hours or days developing proposals to get new projects or jobs, and there is no guarantee that the time they spend will actually lead to work. Either way, it is unpaid time and time away from the projects they already have.

Gig workers find that assignments often come in waves, resulting in feeling pressured to work long hours to complete tasks.

Self-Discipline

As a freelancer, you will have a lot of freedom. But this comes with responsibility. In order to provide a stable income, it is up to you to decide what work needs to be done and when. Freelancers must find good clients and projects they can do well. Tech freelancer Adam Sinicki says, "If you're going to freelance then you need to be disciplined. That means you need to be able to shut the world out and go to town on that website backend/search engine optimization (SEO) content."

Working from home, whether you're an employee or a gig worker, can be challenging. Distractions are everywhere. "You need to be able to avoid the temptation to take breaks whenever you feel like it, and it means you need to stay self-motivated in order to meet deadlines," Sinicki says. Freelancers must adopt a professional mindset because there will be times when work is not appealing. Sinicki suggests, "If you can't imagine working from home without being tempted to give up and play computer games, then perhaps this lifestyle isn't for you."

Self-discipline is something that can be learned. Sinicki notes, "Discipline is something that can be practiced and that will improve with time."

Adam Sinicki, *Thriving in the Gig Economy: Freelancing Online for Tech Professionals and Entrepreneurs*. New York: Apress, 2019, p. 8.

Strange as it may sound, having too many projects can be almost as difficult as having too few. Even when gig workers have a lot of work, many still don't want to turn anything down, knowing there may be times ahead with no work. So they often end up working in spurts of long hours followed by lots of down time, then more long hours, followed again by more down time. It can be hard to get used to these up-and-down cycles. Freelance developer ptrnyc notes, "When they say that freelancing is flexibility, it works both ways. If you want the jobs, you need to be flexible. Sometimes that means 100 hour weeks because you want 2 clients and they both want full-time."[35] When freelancers have way more work than they can realistically do in the agreed-on time frame, it makes for unhappy clients—and unhappy clients tend to go elsewhere for their next project. Although it can be challenging, part of the work of self-employment is to smooth out the ups and downs of both the amount of work and the income as much as possible.

The Business Aspects

Working in the gig economy is being in business for yourself. Freelancers have to learn all aspects of being in business. This means learning to keep detailed records of work done and work remaining. It means tracking and documenting expenses in connection with contracted work. It means learning to read and understand contracts. It means being aware of tax requirements for gig work—or hiring a knowledgeable person or company to help with that. It means planning for the future, both for lean times and when work is plentiful.

Some gig workers are able to invest the time and energy to learn all of these aspects of running a business, but others find it extremely challenging to do this work. Not investing that time can create problems down the road. Becca Kennedy advises that new freelancers "learn all about money and finances! Learn how to price your work, how to pay taxes, and how to manage accounts like health insurance and retirement savings." As a freelancer you will need to set aside money for things like taxes, savings, and health insurance. Learning to manage the business aspects of self-employment helps freelancers thrive. And there are additional rewards: Kennedy notes, "Having those securities in place and building up an emergency fund lets you be more selective about work, giving you the freedom you want."[36]

No Benefits or Worker Protections

Aside from the inconsistency of work and income for gig workers in all fields—tech included—the next biggest worry is lack of benefits. Gig workers typically do not have any of the ben-

Taking the time to learn the ins and outs of business can pay off for the freelance gig worker, who must not only be a tech person but a businessperson as well.

efits that employees in many companies receive. Gig workers do not have paid sick leave. If a family member is sick (or if the gig worker is sick and can't work), there is no one else to pick up the slack. A day without work means a day without pay. Nor do gig workers have paid vacation days or holidays. They do not get overtime pay and generally are not eligible for unemployment benefits. They do not have the option of participating in a 401(k) retirement plan. And if they want health insurance, they have to get it on their own—or go without. According to a 2022 survey by the online benefits platform Stride Health, many gig workers have chosen to go without. The survey revealed that 24 percent of gig workers have no health insurance. More than half of those workers (58 percent) said they did not have insurance because they could not afford it.

Health insurance is an additional monthly expense that can add up to thousands of dollars a year. In response to a question on Reddit, one man who described himself and his wife as freelancers

Health Insurance

Lack of health insurance is an issue for most gig workers. Health insurance and health care are expensive. While some may be able to pay for health insurance through their parents or a partner's employer, other freelancers risk going without insurance. On Reddit, a freelance software developer commented, "Having just come off of 6 years of no insurance, let me be perfectly frank with you: Paying $600/month for insurance is frustrating as heck, but I guarantee you you'll be happy you were paying it if you have something catastrophic happen. 90% of our non-mortgage debt is from medical bills."

He and his wife have children, and even with insurance, the costs of health care add up. He says, "The most recent ER visit we did, where the kid in question just needed [to be] observed for an hour before being sent home? $1500. The one before that, where the kid needed sutures? $3000. The one before that, where the kid had horrible, crippling stomach pains, and needed a CT to rule out something truly nasty? Over $10000." Though high-tech freelancers can earn higher than average pay, factor in costs like health insurance.

inceptivecss, "Health Insurance Is Extremely Expensive and I'm Really Trying to Justify the Cost," Reddit, November 1, 2021. www.reddit.com.

wrote that their health insurance is "expensive enough to make a grown man sit down and cry." For an average plan, he says, "we pay something in the neighborhood of $1300/month for the two of us."[37]

The same survey found that many gig workers are unaware of health insurance that can be obtained through the Affordable Care Act, more commonly known as Obamacare. Many of these workers might be able to obtain lower-cost or subsidized plans this way. However, even when they qualify for these plans, there may be costs. Paul Dodson of Liberty, Tennessee, lost his job as an adjunct chemistry instructor but decided to keep the health care coverage from his former employer because of his chronic back problems. That insurance cost him $1,175 a month. Eventually, he found a more affordable plan through Obamacare. He pays $300 a month, which still takes a chunk of his savings but not nearly as much as before. He says, "The gig economy? Those two words sum everything up. Now I'm driving a little Uber just to make ends meet." However, of the new health plan, he adds, "It's saved my life."[38]

Working with Clients

There are other challenges for those who work in the gig economy. Strong communication skills are essential, but not all gig workers have these skills. For many people, a big part of the appeal of high-tech gig work is that they can work on their own—without being burdened by meetings, email threads, and chitchat with colleagues. While some of this might prove true, the fact is that good communication with current and potential clients is necessary for gig workers in high-tech and programming fields. Adam Sinicki says that in the gig economy, "it's not enough to be a [tech worker], you also have to be a marketer, a complaints department, and an administrator." He admits that "this won't always come easily, especially when it means that focused flow ends up being interrupted by clients asking questions, wanting [changes], or asking for invoices." But he counsels, "Don't think of this as an irritation. Your communication is actually *part* of the service you provide. And it will make a huge difference to the experience of your clients and therefore their likelihood of recommending your services and using them again."[39] Repeat clients and recommendations help a freelancer thrive.

One common communication issue for freelancers is coming to a clear understanding about what work is included in the project. As freelance data scientist Ethan Rosenthal explains, "Sometimes clients have an idea for what they want me to build ('we want to forecast this thing every night'). Other times, clients simply have a problem, and I come up with a solution to this problem." For clarity, Rosenthal writes a "proposal about the requirements and [his] approach for building the machine learning system." Then he works with the client to make a written agreement for the project. If the client later asks for additional work that was not in the original agreement, he says, "requested changes can be clearly demarcated as 'out-of-scope,'"[40] requiring additional payment for the additional work.

Being Social

One attractive feature of gig work is not having to commute to the same building every day, not working predetermined hours, and not being forced to adhere to a particular company's culture. But there are trade-offs for this independence. One of the trade-offs is that you have a lot less interaction with colleagues and other

Whereas gig work allows one to avoid traffic commutes like this one in Seattle, Washington, it also reduces the opportunities of working alongside others.

people in the industry. This can make it harder to develop business relationships.

During his career as a freelance software developer, Sinicki has spent a lot of time working alone. This is the norm, he says. "You'll be working on your own much of the time. That means a lot of isolation." Some people thrive on working alone. They are more productive and more engaged than they would be if they were working for a company. And they have no problem cultivating relationships outside of work. This doesn't work for everyone, however. "For some people, being part of a 'team' is one of the big perks of work,"[41] Sinicki adds. For these individuals, gig work can be very challenging.

While the benefits of working in the gig economy can be appealing, to make it all work, techs must be able to manage the downsides too. Many experienced freelancers recommend starting with side jobs or plenty of savings to cushion the ups and downs of beginning a freelance career. There is a lot to attend to with the work itself and learning about being self-employed. A freelancer can earn great rewards but must exchange that for greater risks.

CHAPTER FIVE

Making a Go of It

Tech evolves rapidly, and job descriptions and skill sets are being created to go along with it. For Becca Kennedy, finding her career path meant creating it in part. Her journey started with education. As a psychology major, she says, "I learned about the field called human factors psychology, which is the study of designing systems to fit humans. It was a true ah-ha moment, and I jumped straight into a PhD program." Many tech fields require a lot of education, and Kennedy notes that her graduate education "took a long time and involved a lot of stress, but eventually I was an expert in human research."[42]

She says she decided UX was "a perfect real-world application of my academic work." But at the time in her town, there were no potential employers. So she decided to work independently. She learned to network and to pitch her services to clients. Kennedy notes, "It can take a lot of time, perseverance, and trial and error." Her work paid off, she says. "It took a few years to build up a portfolio of UX projects, but eventually it worked! I began by offering usability testing because that was close to my academic research experience. Then I slowly moved toward more creative, exploratory work that I felt more excited to do."[43]

Now as a design research consultant, Kennedy leads efforts to help organizations strategize how to make products and services better for users. She says she has become a niche expert, allowing her to "say yes to opportunities that specifically align with my values, priorities, and interests."[44]

Gig Economy Options

Just as there are many different high-tech and programming careers, there are many ways to work independently in those careers. A contractor may work side by side with permanent employees at the organization's office or be completely location independent. Independent work can mean anything from becoming an independent maker of software products to working in traditional employment and doing gigs on the side. Some freelancers build their self-employment business with the goal of becoming a start-up company, learning a lot along the way.

Though some, like Kennedy, launch a consultancy from the start, it is not unusual for people to move fluidly between traditional jobs and alternative employment. According to freelance developer Bennett Garner, independent work does not hurt your chances for future full-time employment. He adds, "There's tons of room for you to pursue your interests before returning to full-time work. The bonus: You may really enjoy and be good at freelancing!"[45]

For those who eventually decide to return to traditional employment, having self-employment experience can be an asset. It shows you've experienced aspects of running a business. And there are other benefits to one's skill set. Garner notes, "Freelancing introduced me to many different projects, problems, and approaches. I learned a ton from seeing how different companies solve various problems."[46]

Nontraditional employment doesn't work for everyone. But for those who thrive on it and can manage the business aspects, Garner says, "it can be quite lucrative. Some people love business ownership so much, they can never imagine going back to work."[47]

Sometimes a gig worker may work side-by-side with an organization's full-time employees to complete a project.

Side Gigs

Having income gives a tech more freedom and spontaneity in pursuing projects. It enabled one independent software developer to take a quick side job while freelancing. He notes that "when you have total freedom over your time, you can decide to briefly use your time on sporadic interesting opportunities." For instance, his friends had a Web3 project. (Web3 uses blockchain technology and AI to store internet data and prevent misuse.) He was interested in this project, and since he was successfully freelancing, he says he was able to "put what I was doing on hold for a few weeks to take on that project, and resume normal operations once it was finished."[48]

Others do side hustles to earn extra money. There is even a movement called FIRE—financial independence, retire early—which suggests that by living frugally and earning higher incomes, high-tech workers have the possibility to save enough money to retire years early.

In an uncertain economy, doing side projects can also be a way to cushion against potential job loss. A reporter for the online news site Vox interviewed side start-up founders. Many felt their employers would not hesitate to fire them or lay them off if it suited their corporate needs. One forty-six-year-old software engineer who is working on a tech side gig of his own says there's a high likelihood that his job will be given to someone who can be paid less. This software engineer and other tech workers who are developing side gigs noted that the start-up possibility is a way to achieve more control over their situations.

Full-stack developer Adam Wathan has been working on projects since he was eight years old, making video game walk-throughs. In these walk-through videos, people show step-by-step how to surmount certain challenges in a video game or even how to play through the entire game from start to finish. Wathan says, "I've always loved the feeling of creating something neat

A Workation

For software engineer Alexander Repty, one of the perks of being an independent software engineer is that he can work almost anywhere. He can even work while on vacation. During his first "workation," he says, "I was working on a freelance contract for a team at Apple which gave me a great deal of autonomy over when I would work during the day." He traveled with his family in a camper and set up a five- to six-hour workday to allow for family time. "I would get to work right after breakfast and work until lunch. . . . After lunch came family time until it became time to prepare for dinner, after which I performed my second chunk of work until that was done." While he worked, his family visited nearby playgrounds and a farm where children could visit farm animals and play in the hay barn. His family loved it, and he says, "We are beyond excited that we did this and how much we've learned from this. The whole experience was a major success."

Alexander Repty, "Going on a Family Workation in a Camping Trailer," Medium, April 26, 2019. https://medium.com.

and polished and putting it out into the world."[49] While working full time, he worked on projects and began blogging. He decided to write a short book on PHP programming. (PHP is a scripting language used for web development.) As he wrote, he posted chapters to his audience for feedback and made improvements. When he released the final book, it was so successful that he quit his job to focus on his projects.

Many of his gigs failed, but Wathan kept trying. He "builds in public," meaning he posted his programming work online as he went along, inviting comments and continuing to improve it. Taking the feedback he received on his work, he eventually built a program to help developers with Cascading Style Sheets (instructions for how web content displays on a site). Five months later Wathan's program had earned almost $2 million. He continues to work on the program and add features.

Layoffs Inspire New Gigs

Mass tech layoffs are changing work for thousands of workers. With valuable skills, laid-off workers are finding new jobs, sometimes in smaller companies or in different industries. Others are deciding to work for themselves. Henry Kirk was one of twelve thousand employees laid off by Google in January 2023. Google gave Kirk a severance package. Severance is compensation for losing a job and can be pay and health benefits for a certain number of months. Kirk is using the severance to pay his bills and start a software design and development service with five other laid-off Google employees. Even with a short window to start bringing in income, Kirk is positive, noting, "My back is against the wall because I have to get back on my feet, [but] I actually am embracing the fact that this happened."[50]

Being laid off from a health care company gave Jen Zhu the opportunity to work on a project creating software to automate some health care industry administrative tasks. She's worked

When Google laid off twelve thousand of its employees in 2023, some received severance packages that gave them the resources to start their own small businesses.

hard and says, "It's a grind. It's really hard to turn off. There's always more to do."[51] Recently, Zhu was one of seven applicants from a pool of twelve hundred who received $100,000 in funding from investors.

Quitting Traditional Jobs to Pursue Passion Projects

Traditional employment in the tech industry can seem like a pretty cushy job, especially when companies offer employee perks such as catered meals, gyms, higher pay, and stock options. These benefits are going away at some companies, another aspect that is adding to the number of people leaving traditional employment.

With many systems deployed online around the clock, it is not unusual for software engineers to work long hours at times and to be on call. "On call" means that if there's an issue during off hours, such as on a Sunday, the engineers may be called on

From Side Projects to Successful Business

While not everyone is passionate about their work, the flexibility of gig work can allow time for a passion project—or the gig itself can be a passion project. Some passion projects become successful businesses. Joost de Valk worked at several positions in tech while creating programs on the side called plug-ins. The plug-ins provide new functionality for WordPress. WordPress is open-source software for building simple websites. It is used by 38 million sites worldwide.

After creating and refining different plug-ins, de Valk's Yoast SEO (search engine optimization) plug-in took off. The plug-in helps website owners make their sites more discoverable by search engines. Now the Yoast SEO plug-in runs on more than 12 million websites and 16 percent of the 1 million most-visited sites worldwide, according to BuiltWith, which researches which technologies websites use. In an interview, de Valk shared this advice: "The single most important thing is to do what you love. . . . The reason for that is simple: love for what you do will make your work not feel like work."

Quoted in Editorial Team, "Joost de Valk, Founder of Yoast, Shares His Success Story," 1stWebDesigner, April 26, 2016. https://1stwebdesigner.com.

to resolve it. In addition to occasional long hours, because some workers are experiencing layoffs, there is a level of job insecurity for those who remain. And with fewer coworkers, those remaining bear an increased burden to develop and maintain systems. As Elon Musk laid off thousands at Twitter, he declared that techs must "work 12 hours a day, 7 days a week, or else you're fired."[52] That is an extreme case, but the workplace is changing for some high-tech workers, leading some to quit traditional employment to pursue projects that interest them.

In 2022 software engineer Nish Junankar was working for OpenSea, a non-fungible token (NFT) marketplace. NFTs are crypto assets that use blockchain technology to verify ownership, such as of a video game character or digital artwork. When layoffs started that year, unlike many of his coworkers, Junankar was offered a retention package. A retention package is a way to entice a key employee to stay on with a company and often includes a cash bonus, salary increase, and other benefits. Concerned that he would be expected to take on more responsibilities and work longer hours to make up for the laid-off employees, he opted to leave the company and start his own tech gig.

He's working on developing a home furnishings platform. In addition to developing the software, Junankar is looking for investors. He says, "It's incredibly stressful." There is a lot of preparation for the investor presentations, and meanwhile he is burning through cash provided by family and friends who believe in him and his idea. Despite the pressure, Junankar says, "it's incredibly rewarding and fulfilling. It doesn't feel like work."[53]

Some workers see being laid off as an opportunity to try something new and start rounding up investors for their own new company.

Tech Talent and the Gig Economy

Even with the recent instability in the tech field, according to tech research firm Gartner, "The tech talent crunch is far from over. Current demand for tech talent greatly outstrips supply, which Gartner expects will be the case until at least 2026."[54] The demand means there will continue to be freelancing opportunities. In the gig economy, freelancers can choose to be selective about projects they take on. Independent workers can experience greater creativity and autonomy in completing work and can choose to devote time to their own projects. Tech gigs offer an opportunity to earn higher-than-average pay, contribute and learn, and tackle challenges. There may be chances to work remotely. For freelancers in high-tech and programming careers, strong demand for their skills gives them enviable options to truly explore what they are capable of.

SOURCE NOTES

Introduction: Gig Work in High Tech and Programming

1. Heather Joslyn and Jennifer Riggins, "How Will Working in Tech Change in 2023?," New Stack, January 10, 2023. https://thenewstack.io.
2. Quoted in Emily Sullivan, "Voices of America's Contract Workers: 'I Love the Freedom,'" NPR, January 22, 2018. www.npr.org.
3. Quoted in Reddit, "How Did You Make Your First $20 Freelancing?," February 18, 2019. www.reddit.com.

Chapter One: Tech Work in the Gig Economy

4. Larry W., interview with the author, January 10, 2023.
5. Daniel Bourke, *I Left My Machine Learning Job—Ask Me Anything*, YouTube, June 29, 2019. www.youtube.com/watch?v=w1g8-t0EXXY.
6. Heather, interview with the author, January 8, 2023.
7. Nick D., interview with the author, January 11, 2023.
8. Brad Traversy, "Freelancing as a Web Developer," Traversy Media, February 27, 2018. https://www.youtube.com/watch?v=m2N3tmJ_A0Q.
9. Quoted in Amanda Hoover, "Big Tech Laid Off Thousands. Here's Who Wants Them Next," *Wired*, December 16, 2022. www.wired.com.

Chapter Two: Breaking into the High-Tech and Programming Gig Economy

10. Larry W., interview.
11. Larry W., interview.
12. Adam Sinicki, "How to Work as a Software Developer Online: Everything You Need to Know," Android Authority, June 30, 2019. www.androidauthority.com.
13. Alex Suzuki, "Going Freelance as a Software Engineer—Some Advice," Medium, February 4, 2019. https://medium.com.
14. Quoted in Reddit, "I Fell for a Job Scam and Now I Feel Completely Defeated in My Search," February 24, 2023. www.reddit.com.

15. Quoted in Reddit, "I Fell for a Job Scam and Now I Feel Completely Defeated in My Search."
16. Strategic Analyst, "Be Prepared to Be Tracked and Working Exactly 40hrs," Glassdoor, November 26, 2021. www.glassdoor.com.

Chapter Three: The Upsides of Gig Work

17. Adam Sinicki, *Thriving in the Gig Economy: Freelancing Online for Tech Professionals and Entrepreneurs*. New York: Apress, 2019, p. xiii.
18. Adam Sinicki, "What is the Gig Economy? Why the Future of Work Is Online (and How to Prepare)," Android Authority, May 15, 2021. www.androidauthority.com.
19. Ethan Rosenthal, "Doing Freelance Data Science Consulting in 2019," Ethan Rosenthal personal website, January 8, 2020. www.ethanrosentha.com.
20. Sinicki, *Thriving in the Gig Economy*, p. 3.
21. Heather, interview.
22. Andrew Van Dam, "The Happiest, Least Stressful, Most Meaningful Jobs in America," *Washington Post*, January 6, 2023. www.washingtonpost.com.
23. Karla L. Miller, "Work Advice: My Employer Is Reneging on Its Remote-Work Promise," *Washington Post*, February 2, 2023. www.washingtonpost.com.
24. Quoted in Karla L. Miller, "He's Been Diagnosed with Autism. Is It Too Late to Keep His Job?," *Washington Post*, October 13, 2022. www.washingtonpost.com.
25. Becca Kennedy, interview with the author, February 28, 2023. www.beccakennedy.net.
26. MakeMyMove, "Do What You Love, in a Place That You Love," 2023. www.makemymove.com.
27. Quoted in Gianpiero Petriglieri et al., "Thriving in the Gig Economy," *Harvard Business Review*, March–April 2018. https://hbr.org.
28. Kennedy, interview.
29. Nick D., interview.
30. Quoted in Reddit, "Why Freelancing Is Different than I Expected," November 6, 2020. www.reddit.com.
31. Quoted in Reddit, "To Be a Successful Web Developer You Need to Learn How to Learn," September 30, 2020. www.reddit.com.

Chapter Four: The Downsides of Gig Work

32. Quoted in Reddit, "Why Freelancing Is Different than I Expected."
33. Quoted in Paul Davidson, "Layoffs, Recession Fears Spur Some Companies to Hire More Gig Economy Workers," *USA Today*, March 1, 2023. www.usatoday.com.
34. Quoted in Quora, "If You're a Full-Time Freelancer, Do You Work on Weekends Too? Do You Have Any Days Off?," 2020. www.quora.com.

35. Quoted in Reddit, "How to Look for Part Time Freelance Work. Is It Even Possible?," March 6, 2023. www.reddit.com.
36. Kennedy, interview.
37. Quoted in Reddit, "Freelancers in America, What Is Your Health Insurance Situation?," July 19, 2019. www.reddit.com.
38. Quoted in Blake Farmer, "Gig Workers Are Signing Up for ACA Health Benefits, Though Many Still Go Uncovered," Marketplace, November 21, 2022. www.marketplace.org.
39. Sinicki, *Thriving in the Gig Economy*, p. 99.
40. Rosenthal, "Doing Freelance Data Science Consulting in 2019."
41. Sinicki, *Thriving in the Gig Economy*, p. 9.

Chapter Five: Making a Go of It

42. Kennedy, interview.
43. Kennedy, interview.
44. Kennedy, interview.
45. Bennett Garner, "Does Freelancing Kill Your Developer Career?," Developer Purpose, September 19, 2022. https://blog.developerpurpose.com.
46. Garner, "Does Freelancing Kill Your Developer Career?"
47. Garner, "Does Freelancing Kill Your Developer Career?"
48. Rameerez, "What Is an Indie Hacker?—A Guide to Indie Hacking," Rameerez personal website, February 19, 2022. https://rameerez.com.
49. Adam Wathan, "The $61,392 Book Launch That Let Me Quit My Job," Adam Wathan personal website, April 21, 2017. https://adamwathan.me.
50. Quoted in Amanda Hoover, "Tech Layoffs Are Feeding a New Startup Surge," *Wired*, February 22, 2023. www.wired.com.
51. Quoted in Hoover, "Tech Layoffs Are Feeding a New Startup Surge."
52. Quoted in Mehul Reuben Das, "Elon Musk to Twitter Employees: 'Work 12 Hours a Day, 7 Days Every Week or Else You're Fired,'" Firstpost, November 3, 2022. www.firstpost.com.
53. Quoted in Hoover, "Tech Layoffs Are Feeding a New Startup Surge."
54. Mbula Schoen, "Do Recent Layoffs Mean the Tech Talent Crunch Is Over?," Gartner, March 7, 2023. www.gartner.com.

INTERVIEW WITH A SOLUTION/SOFTWARE ARCHITECT

Nuri Bal has worked as a freelance solution/software architect since 2018. He also worked as a contractor on various software projects in Silicon Valley for eight years. Like many people working in the gig economy, he has also worked in a traditional job. Bal currently lives in Hamburg, Germany. He answered the following questions by email.

Q: Briefly describe your job.
A: I am a software architect for telecom applications. The job does not require any hands-on software development. But the software development background is a must.

Q: Briefly describe a typical workday as a freelancer.
A: Working in an agile environment, we have our daily stand-up meeting for 30 minutes. The rest of the day is spent pretty much on code review, Jira (issue tracking) tickets, system requirements, and interactions with software developers.

Q: How is gig work different from a regular job?
A: The work is spread out to multiple time slices. What I mean by "time slices" is being able to work in small time chunks rather than a 9 to 5 job. I can flexibly work early in the morning for 2 hours, and then enjoy coffee and breakfast time with my wife. I record my billable work time down to 15 min increments in a spreadsheet so that I don't have to guess later. Shopping, exercise, and cooking would fit into my work day which may be up to 5 hours spread around.

There is no company mandate on on-premises work. The customer project we work on behalf of our client gets renewed in 4- to 6-month intervals. So there is work to do only when there is [a] customer purchase order. Otherwise we are off taking a break from work.

Q: Why did you decide to do gig work?
A: I cannot picture myself working 8 hours a day on fixed salary with minimal vacation time.

Q: What do you like most about working in the gig economy?
A: Flexibility and freedom.

Q: What do you like least about working in the gig economy?
A: I wish I had a chance to go into the office once in a while.

Q: What personal qualities are important for working in the gig economy?
A: Self-discipline, attention to details, focus, customer/client friendly, and a desire to reach perfection.

Q: What advice do you have for students who want to work in the gig economy?
A: Get curious about new technologies, software skills, life skills, software automation, and improve your communication skills.

FIND OUT MORE

Internet Sources

Kristen Dalli, "IRS Shares Tax Tips for Gig Economy Workers: Paying Estimated Taxes Throughout the Year May Be Helpful for These Workers," Consumer Affairs, January 17, 2023. www.consumeraffairs.com.

Brittany Lambert et al., "Employees Are Fighting Hard to Keep Working Remotely—but It Can Come with a High Emotional Cost. 4 Experts Draw on Gig Work Research to Offer Practical Advice," *Fortune*, January 4, 2023. https://fortune.com.

Jennifer Liu, "Some Cities Are Paying People up to $16,000 to Move There—This Online Directory Will Help You Find Them," CNBC, March 16, 2021. www.cnbc.com.

Clément Mihailescu, *Google Coding Interview with a High School Student*, YouTube, May 3, 2020. www.youtube.com/watch?v=qz9tKlF431k.

Michael Rosen, "Tips to Help Gig Workers Stay Healthy," *New Hampshire Union Leader* (Manchester, NH), January 19, 2023. www.unionleader.com.

Amira Sounny-Slitine, "Gig Economy: What Is It and How Does It Work?," Indeed, March 30, 2021. www.indeed.com.

Websites

The Balance

www.thebalancemoney.com
This site provides small business basics, including office setup, business taxes, banking, and insurance. Elsewhere on the site is general information and tips about working in

the gig economy, advantages, disadvantages, and getting started, as well as career guidance, skills development, résumés, and interviews.

Bureau of Labor Statistics *Occupational Outlook Handbook*
www.bls.gov/ooh
The Bureau of Labor Statistics researches and compiles data about the US workforce. The Occupational Outlook Handbook is a trove of information about jobs, including what they do, how to prepare, work environment, pay, future job outlook, and more.

Khan Academy
www.khanacademy.org
This is a nonprofit organization providing free online educational courses for all ages, including children and teens. Khan Academy offers free online classes in math, science, computing, and other subjects.

MakeMyMove
www.makemymove.com
This site shows places that will pay remote workers to move there. Search by offer, location, or amenity (outdoor life, college town, small town feel, and so on).

Stack Overflow
www.stackoverflow.com
Stack Overflow is a website for the tech community, providing a place to debug code, ask questions, and do research.

Women in Data Science (WiDS)
www.ischool.berkeley.edu/events/2022/wids-berkeley
WiDS is an international community offering conferences, lectures, seminars, datathons, podcasts, and blogs. The Next Gen program is an initiative of Women in Data Science that supports high school students.

Videos

Forrest Knight, *What Professional Software Engineers ACTU-ALLY Do*, YouTube, September 28, 2021. www.youtube.com/watch?v=Q0A35ZfgwHA.

Gyasi Linje, *The Harsh Reality of Being a Software Engineer*, YouTube, November 11, 2021. www.youtube.com/watch?v=Ws6zCMdp9Es.

STEM Programs for Young People

AI4ALL
https://ai4all.princeton.edu
AI4ALL offers an annual summer camp to teach AI to high school students from underrepresented groups. The camps are open to promising eleventh graders. Grants to cover the cost of the three-week program on the Princeton University campus are based on need.

Girls Who Code (GWC)
https://girlswhocode.com/programs/summer-immersion-program
GWC is a nonprofit that offers free summer and school-year computer science programs and invites girls, women, and nonbinary individuals to apply.

Howard University High School Summer Enrichment Programs
https://business.howard.edu/office-student-affairs/high-school-summer-enrichment-programs
This is a free, one-week summer program for students in grades 10 and 11. Students live on campus, and choose from one of four areas: accounting, information systems, actuarial science, and entrepreneurship.

**National Institute of Standards and Technology
Summer High School Intern Program**
www.nist.gov/iaao/summer-high-school-intern-program
This is a competitive, eight-week program for paid summer internships in cutting-edge scientific research positions. Students provide their own housing and transportation. Past projects have included labs in communications technology, information technology, and engineering.

Western New York STEM Hub Hand in Hand Program
www.wnystem.org/hand-in-hand
Middle and high school youth in this program use technology and computer design to build prosthetic hands for children in need. The summer program is in August.

INDEX

Note: Boldface page numbers indicate illustrations.

Affordable Care Act (Obamacare), 40–41
Alexa, building apps for, 20
All Tech Is Human (job board), 24
Arkonovich, Steven, 20
assistive technology, 9

Balance, The (website), 58–59
blockchain architecture, 13–14
Boston University, 18
Bourke, Daniel, 10
BuiltWith, 50
Bureau of Labor Statistics, 7, 28, 59

certifications, 18–19
communication skills, 41
computer vision, 10
Computing Technology Industry Association, 19
Crossover (freelancing platform), 22
cybersecurity, 8

data engineer, 7
data scientist, 9–10, 27, 41–42
digital nomads, 30–31
Dodson, Paul, 40–41
Doughty, Sam, 9
downside of gig work
    challenges of working with clients as, 41–42
    getting work and, 35–38
    job scams and, 21–22

lack of benefits/worker protections as, 38–41
managing a business as, 38
social isolation as, 42–43

earnings/income, 40, 52
    on gig platforms, 22
    for tech jobs, 13–14
    uncertainty with, 35–36
education/training programs
    certification for, 19
    college/internships and, 18
    STEM classes and, 16–17
    summer opportunities for, 17–18
    tutorials as, 18
enterprise architect, 7

Fast Company, 15
Freelancer (freelancing platform), 22
freelancing platforms, 22–24
full stack engineer/developer, 7, 22, 47
Future Forum, 32

Garner, Bennett, 45
Gartner (research firm), 52
gig work/gig economy
    for neurodivergent individuals, 29–30
    reasons for taking, **5**
    rise of, 4–5
    See also downside of gig work; upside of gig work
Gilbert, Tina, 32
GitHub, 20

Glassdoor (job search site), 7, **8**

Harvard Business Review (journal), 32–33
health insurance, 38, 39–41
Hodgson, Lindsay, 4–5
Howard University, 18
Humphrey, Elias, 9

insurance
   as high-stress industry, 28
   See also health insurance
internships, 18

Java developer, 7
job boards, 24–25
job scams, 21–22
Joslyn, Heather, 4
Junankar, Nish, 50–51

Kennedy, Becca, 30, 33, 38
   on creating a career path, 44–45
Khan Academy (website), 17, 59
Kirk, Henry, 48
knowledge workers, 8, 15

LinkedIn (online job board), 18

machine learning/machine learning engineer, 7, 10, 13
MakeMyMove (website), 31, 59
Miller, Karla, 32
Munitz, Jon, 36
Musk, Elon, 50

National Initiative for Cybersecurity Education (NICE), 8, 18
neurodiversity, 29–30

Occupational Outlook Handbook (Bureau of Labor Statistics), 59
operations engineer, 7
opinion polls. *See* surveys

PHP programming, 48

Pollfish, 15
polls. *See* surveys
Program in Mathematics for Young Scientists (Boston University), 18
PythonDevs (reverse job board), 24

RailsDevs (reverse job board), 24
Repty, Alexander, 47
research mathematician, 10, 12, 16
retirement savings, 38
reverse job boards, 24–25
Riddle, Joseph, 29–30
Riggins, Jennifer, 4
robotics, average pay for, 14
Rosenthal, Ethan, 27, 41–42
Ross Mathematics Program (Indiana), 18

side projects, 47
Sinicki, Adam, 20
   on need for self-discipline, 37
   on social isolation, 43
   on upsides of gig work, 26, 27
   on working with clients, 41
social isolation, 42–43
software developer/engineer, 7, 40, 46, 47
   open-source projects and, 20
   on programming, 34
   reverse job boards for, 24
   on starting out, 35
solution/software architect, interview with, 56–57
Stack Overflow (job board), 24, 59
STEM (science, technology, engineering, and math) education, 16–17
stress, in STEM careers, 28–29
Stride Health (online benefits platform), 39
surveys
   on freelance work and job stability, 15
   of gig workers on health insurance, 39

Suzuki, Alex, 21

tech jobs
    earnings for, 13–14
    reliability/stability of, 14–15
Tech Jobs for Good (job board), 24
technical writer, 11–13
Toptal (freelancing platform), 22
Twitter (social media platform), 50

University of Chicago, 18
upside of gig work
    ability to try new lines of work as,
        33–34
    ability to work remotely as, 29–31
    flexibility as, 24–28, 30
    having meaningful work as, 32–33
    less stress as, 28–29
    travel as, 47
Upwork (freelancing platform), 22

US Digital Response (job board),
    24
user experience (UX) researcher,
    10–11

Valk, Joost de, 50
Van Dam, Andrew, 28
virtual reality, average pay for, 14
voice apps, 20

Wathan, Adam, 47–48
Web3, 46
Williams, Kesha, 20
Women in Data Science (WiDS), 59
WordPress, 50

Young Scholars Program (University
    of Chicago), 18

Zhu, Jen, 48–49